Magical Essays & Instructions

By Florence Farr

Copyright © 2019 Lamp of Trismegistus. All rights reserved. No part of this publication may be reproduced or transmitted in any form or by any means, electronic or mechanical, including photocopying, recording, or by any information storage and retrieval system, without permission in writing from Lamp of Trismegistus. Reviewers may quote brief passages.

ISBN: 978-1-63118-418-5

Esoteric Classics

Other Books in this Series and Related Titles

The Human Aura: Astral Colors and Thought Forms
by Swami Panchadasi and William Walker Atkinson
(978-1-63118-419-2)

Ancient Mysteries and Secret Societies by Manly P. Hall
(978-1-63118-410-9)

The First and Second Gospels of the Infancy of Jesus Christ
by Thomas and James (978-1-63118-415-4)

The Book of the Watchers by Enoch
(978-1-63118-416-1)

The Story and Legend of Hiram Abiff
by William Harvey, Manly P. Hall and Albert G. Mackey
(978-1-63118-411-6)

Rosa Alchemica, The Tables of Law & The Adoration of the Magi
by William Butler Yeats (978-1-63118-421-5)

The Philosophy of Masonry in Five Parts by Roscoe Pound
(978-1-63118-004-0)

Occult Symbolism of Animals, Insects, Reptiles, Fish and Birds
by Manly P. Hall (978-1-63118-420-8)

The Lives of Adam and Eve by Moses (978-1-63118-414-7)

A Collection of Writings Related to Occult, Esoteric, Rosicrucian and Hermetic Literature, Including Freemasonry, the Kabbalah, the Tarot, Alchemy and Theosophy various authors *Volumes 1-4*
(978-1-63118-713-1) (978-1-63118-714-8)
(978-1-63118-715-5) (978-1-63118-716-2)

Audio Versions are also Available on Audible and iTunes

Table of Contents

Introduction...7

The Magic of a Symbol...9

On the Play of the Image-Maker...29

The Tetrad or The Structure of the Mind...37

Egyptian Use of Symbols...49

The Philosophy Called Vedanta...57

On the Kabbalah...67

The Rosicrucians and the Alchemists...77

Introduction

The word "esoteric" can be difficult to define. Esotericism in general can be seen less as a system of beliefs and more as a category, which encompasses numerous, different systems of beliefs. It's a bit of juxtaposition, since the word "esoteric" indicates something that few people know about, while the term itself broadly covers numerous philosophies, practices, areas of study and belief systems.

In a greater sense, Esotericism acts as a storehouse for secret knowledge, which is often considered ancient (by *tradition, if not by fact),* passed down from generation to generation, in private. At various times in history, simply possessing the knowledge of some of these subjects, was considered illegal and a jailable offence, if discovered. This usually included such general topics as Alchemy, Qabalah, Hermeticism, Occultism, Ceremonial Magic, Astrology, Divination, Rosicrucianism and so on. Collectively, these areas of study were often referred to as the esoteric sciences.

Sometimes, the outer garment of a subject isn't esoteric, while what is hidden beneath it, is. As an example, Freemasonry isn't necessarily esoteric by nature (at *least not anymore),* but certain signs, passwords and handshakes given to the candidate during their initiation, are in fact, esoteric, in the sense that they are hidden from the general public.

Today, in the twenty-first century, such topics are readily available at bookstores across the country, and numerous mainsteam publishers offer beginners guides and coffee-table volumes on many of these subjects, intended for mass appeal. Books like *"The Secret"* have turned previously arcane topics into household knowledge. All that being the case, however, it isn't to say that there still aren't buried secrets to uncover, ancient wisdom being ignored and forgotten mysteries to be explored. In fact, it is often that we are only able to further our own studies by standing on the shoulders of these disappearing giants.

Lamp of Trismegistus is doing its part to help preserve humanity's esoteric history by making some of these classics available to those students who are seeking to unearth the knowledge of these ancient colossi.

So, be sure to check other titles from our *Esoteric Classics* series, as well as our *Occult Fiction, Theosophical Classics, Foundations of Freemasonry* and our *Christian Apocrypha Series*.

The Magic of a Symbol

The Japanese, who keep only one beautiful object in each room, know the reward of limiting sense impressions and giving the imagination time to work with the impression it has received. This same reward arises from the use of symbols, for to the mind each impression is a possible symbol of unimagined magnificence. A line of verse, a piece of inlay, may easily sink so deep into the substance of thought that it can take root and grow, for that is the meaning of culture. So, we give our impressions time to grow into trees, that ideas, like birds, may come and sit in their branches.

When the ancients used symbols as objects of meditation they knew this reward given to simple impressions; and I have found that the use of symbols restores to the mind a forgotten power of concentration. They force us to think about a given thing for a considerable period of time and make it impossible to carry on two or three trains of thought at once. They help us to watch our minds at work. If we focus the attention on a symbol we can recall the whole train of imagination and ideas that arise from the symbolic root. In trying to still thought without the use of a symbol the task is still harder, for then irrelevant ideas arise and pass in fantastic pantomime before the eye of the mind, or the memory revolves on some familiar topic in fruitless iteration.

If we focus the attention consecutively on two different symbols we can compare our moods under the different stimuli, for the symbol will give a stimulus towards a mood if it is allowed time to do so. More than this, we can experiment, we can criticize and compare our feelings, when we fix our attention and call up any images without reference to ancient tradition. Or we can use the tradition and, as the ancients did, imagine or regard the symbol of a hawk's eye with the intention of bringing the mind in contact with the keen sight of the bird that can gaze at the sun without dismay.

Again, we might not only wish for sight but for actual power of imagining ourselves to take on characteristics alien to our nature. I am told a great majority of people cannot use their imagination in thinking at all. They cannot sympathize or feel with other creatures or people of different temperaments from their own; they cannot act or pretend to feel what they do not feel; they cannot see what others are like enough even to make a caricature of them. Many people can never describe a person or an event in words, and very often they cannot even express their own thoughts. These people have vague feelings of attraction or repulsion, but no impression that they can express accurately. They are, like the elementary substance, capable of irritation, but not capable of ideas or the expression of ideas. This is partly because of the modern spirit, which demands repletion of every sense and overfeeding both of the mind and body. They do not understand art because they look at too many pictures, or religion because they go to church too often, or music because they attend too many concerts.

When we realize what this state of mind means we do all we can to try and acquire the power of transformation which is above all things necessary to us if our life is to be a human life and not the life of an animal. We must learn to feel with others and to understand them. The Egyptians called the Lord of this discipline of the mind, Kephera, the Transformer. His symbol is the sun at midnight and the scarab. By reducing the mind to the peacefulness of the darkest hour of the night, by sinking into a state in which we for a time forget the eternal "I am" we learn to understand the deeper strata of our "Being."

The wise student who wishes to attain the power and understanding of transformation approaches that realm where the absolute and the relative are seen to be co-existent aspects of the one Being; where the consciousness symbolized by the mathematical point, aware of its unity of substance with all other points, is realized as the ultimate state of all Being, apart from moods and tenses. At the same time all egoisms are perceived to be arrangements of this substance, or rather ideas created by the notion of separateness and form. The symbols of lines, surfaces, solids and spaces are modes or arrangements of these ultimate points. They symbolize consciousness extended in certain directions and drawn in from others.

The use of symbols as a means of focusing the mind and as a means of perceiving abstruse ideas is only touched upon now because all the mystics used them in these ways, as will be pointed out in detail later on.

Let us consider now what we have to take the place of symbols. For it is certain that very few of this generation have ever tried to discipline their thoughts in any way. Sometimes a man here and there becomes aware of the folly of his revolving memory and his wild imaginations, and his only remedy is work. Incessant work silences the folly of thought; but it silences the wisdom of thought also. Why does he not try the effect of wise and ordered thought, and study the structure of his mind? Is it because of the terror that confronts him on the threshold of this adventure? The terror of responsibility?

Most of us will choose any alternative rather than sit still and think until we see clearly as the sun itself that we alone are responsible for what we are. The weight of that terror makes us fly to work, to pleasure, to anything that will crowd our minds with irrelevant things. A man will cover up his own sanctuary with a veil and worship any other god; he will attend ceremonies; he will adore before many altars, but he will not listen to the inner voice. Any other responsibility he will accept, fatherhood, the government of people, the command in battle, but not the responsibility for himself. Or he laughs at life, and reproaches God with his misfortunes. Like Omar he says:

> O thou who didst with pitfall and with gin
> Beset the path I was to wander in,
> For all the sin wherewith the face of man
> Is blackened— man's forgiveness give and take.

"Why was this life of misery ever contrived?" we ask; and those of us who have listened for the answer hear the reply quite clearly: "Because you yourself wearied of the unchangeable bliss of infinite Being, and voluntarily separated yourself in order that the spectacle of life might pass in a panorama before your eyes; you were so enamored of those phantasies that you have almost forgotten whence you came and the way of return is hard to find." When we have heard this answer, we see the reason of many things, and we no longer think life so worthy of reproach.

Then we search for the source of responsible cause, and we watch its first movements as relativity in time and space and growth. We seek for the stable point in Time and find it Now; the stable point in Space and find it Here; the stable point in growth and creation and we find it This. This Here and Now exist everywhere, at all times and under all conditions. The eternal paradox is hidden in these words, for they are ever different but ever present, and both these things together. In the midst of change they subsist as the roots of changing form. The roots of the World-Tree, growth and decay, past and future, form and name, can be concentrated into these three points of This, Here, Now. After all, the World-Tree is a wonderful thing. Why should we not sit among the roots of it with the ancient sages and Death, the Lord of gods? For we are one with them, and it is because we have eaten of the Tree that we forget that we are ourselves That which gave it birth.

When we accept the responsibility, wisdom will come, for it is given as a gift to the wise. When we arise from our illusions and watch deep in our own hearts the inveterate notions of Time and Space and Cause which are the necessities of our ways of thinking, we see them crouching in their lairs waiting to spring out on us or to steal gently and lead us down the long roads which have no ending, and we begin to understand the impostors we so long have harbored as our ideals. Progress is the name of the arch-illusionist, for it is the serpent which tempts us to look ever onward and beyond, instead of waking to the fullest realization here and now. The Utmost and the Highest are within us now if we will but look within and find the great secret of community of Being. But no, the mind refuses to believe it; it desires stimulus for action, it wants to have more, to do more, to be more. It delights in the ebb and flow of change and apparent progress.

Our meditations on real Being may be assisted by the use of mathematical symbols, such as cubes, tetrads, lines, circles, points. For as Leonardo da Vinci says: "Believe nothing till you can reduce it to a mathematical formulary." And mathematical symbols are a great comfort to the searcher after True Being.

But this is only a part of the work of symbols. If they can be a focus for the imagination, they can also be a focus for the will, and they are used by some who desire to awaken their latent powers in order to concentrate attention on the work to be accomplished.

That most mysterious of all moods, the mood of Faith, flourishes sometimes when it is, as it were, watered by the daily recollection of the imagination. And the imagination may be helped by the use of some moving symbol. The wise teacher sometimes uses symbols, just as the priest unveils the symbols of religion before his people that they may receive an influx of the enthusiasm that awakens the potent mood of faith. There are many other times when symbols such as a flag are of enormous value in conveying emotion to a regiment. A crowd is moved by a pageant and by the sight of some representation of dramatic goodness, badness, or heroism. A conjuror acts in the same way and uses symbols with which he is familiar to cast a glamour over the little group of people he is about to delude. And I was told by a young chela that his master had taught him the means of counteracting the symbols used by the jugglers, so that he might not be deceived by the tricks they performed.

These are a few of the uses that have been made of symbols. But I want specially to talk of them as a help to the understanding of our own mystery, and in thinking of magic do not let us associate it with the foolishness of the present age, but rather go back to the real meaning of the word. Magic power only implies a power not limited by common experience, neither is the painting of great pictures nor the writing of great books limited by common experience. Both these things can be achieved only by two or three men in a generation. Magic power was a power given as a gift to those who had diligently set themselves to the work of understanding. "What is this phantom being I call myself?" What mystical Cup is the fountain of its being?

The human soul is very hard to find, very hard even to symbolize, so hard that most of us have given up the quest. It hides from us under fantastic disguises. It appears to one man as his passions, to another as his curiosity, to another as his conscience, to another as his faith. To a few it is known as the source of all these things; and they symbolize it as a fountain or cup.

The creative world of the Kabbalah is symbolized by a cup. The crater, the bowl, the cauldron are all symbolic of plenitude and fecundity. The Quest of the Holy Grail has woven itself into English literature for hundreds of years. Persian mystics interpret the cup to mean the skull, the seat of the imagination; and the wine it contains is the inebriation of the spirit which is the fourth state of mystic meditation.

The Gnostics write of the cup of oblivion given to the souls of men before birth that they may forget their true state; they write also of the cup of wisdom given to the good in order that they may not forget.

According to the Vedanta Philosophy the cup of ignorance (Avidya) is the source of man's separated life. It is the Karana Sharira (creative soul) of a human being, while the creative soul of a god is Maya, the cup of wisdom (vidya or maya). For the Divine Being is aware of the deceptive nature of form in the same way as a skilled juggler is aware that his hands are creating delusion deceptive to his own eyes. But the soul who creates a man enters into his creation, is deluded as it were by his own handiwork, and in this way separates himself by pride from wisdom and enters into ignorance.

Hence there are two cups, the holy cup of Sophia and the profane cup of folly, and on this point the Gnostics and Vedantists are agreed.

According to Hermes Trismegistus the cup or monad is the cup of unity. The initiate plunged his body into the cup of the mind. Baptism is this symbolic plunging of the whole nature into the mind-filled font. In the state of fulfilment called the Pleroma the mind and body are unified in a subtilized body and heaven and earth are mixed therein. The earliest words alluding to the sacramental feast of bread and wine are to be found on the walls of the Pyramid of Unas at Sakara, date about 3700 B.C. The children of the sun were Shu and Tefnut, the divine twin boy and girl. He was symbolized by the white wheaten bread and she by the drink made from the red barley. Her name means the height of the sky whence the Elixir of Life descended upon earth as from an inverted bowl at noon-time. His name meant the light of dawn, and he stands holding up his hands as the separator of light and darkness. As we shall see presently under another symbolic formula he is the Doer, she the Eye of Light or Seer, and these two together are the elements of the cross.

For the present, however, we must keep to our quest of the cup. The next place in which we find it is on some old playing cards called the tarot. These are divining cards and differ a good deal from modern playing cards. The four suits are wands, cups, swords and pentacles, taking the place of diamonds, hearts, spades and clubs. They had somewhat the same symbols among the ancient Irish, who called them the spear, the cauldron, the sword, and the stone. They symbolize fire, water, air and earth; also energy, love, intellect and the physical body. They have been associated with the Tetragrammaton of the Kabbalists, and the worlds of archetype, creation, formation and matter. So that we come to the idea of Eve and creation symbolized by the cups or hearts of playing cards. It is only a year or two ago that the relationship between the suits of cups and hearts appeared in the vision of a seer who imagined his consciousness to enter into a symbolic chamber in the region of the heart and found therein a palace with porphyry pillars and lamps formed like serpents with jeweled lights in their heads and a man holding a cup in his right hand.

In a Vedantic book called the *Yoga Vasishta Laghu* the states of the seeker are divided into seven degrees, and in the last but one the soul is compared to water in a vessel floating in the ocean but protected from the disturbance of storms and tides. The holy man in this degree has made a sanctuary for his soul, a closed place in which he may hold converse with his Being. In the final stage of meditation this vessel is broken, and the soul, which has found its true nature in the cup of holy peace, must remember the truth when it is cast without refuge into the ocean of changing life. In this symbolism the cup serves as a means to an end, for in the state of peaceful meditation the silence is full of ecstasy. It is the cup of the elixir which strengthens the tired soul on its pilgrimage. Like the mythical walled city of gold it is a refuge from the turmoil of change and corruption. But the supreme adventure must be attempted sooner or later, and the soul must resolve to remember always whether doing good or evil, whether seeing beauty or ugliness, that its immortality depends upon its unity with the master of illusion instead of with the slave of illusion. In other words its immortality depends upon its capacity for understanding its own immortal substance. Its substance is eternal, but is not always aware of its own Being, because it is too much aware of its own qualities.

I have already said that it is possible to discipline the mind by the use of symbols used as a focus for the imagination. Let us contemplate a method of this nature.

The devout student has chosen, let us say, the symbol of the Holy Grail. He finds among his treasures an ancient crystal cup and sets it in a shrine. Here when the world is at peace, perhaps in the early hours before dawn, he lights a lamp, burning some sweet-smelling oil, and swings his thurible of incense slowly to and fro. The first degree of the work is to collect the wandering thoughts and fix the whole power of the intellect upon the symbol of his meditation; the second degree is attained when his body has become unwilling to stir; soon afterwards the sense of quietude pervades the whole mind and body. Later on, the mind reaches the fourth degree and becomes inebriated with the store of life gathered into it. It is as if the stilling of the flow of thought had turned the wine into a fire of burning spirit, filling the cup of sacrifice. The fifth degree is the absolute stilling of all thoughts and images, and the symbol is forgotten in the great expanses of formless exultation. The sixth is the degree of privation; terror and anguish attend the pilgrim as he is passing to the higher degrees of consciousness. Pride is the gate which shuts him out from these; pride in his own powers and attainments and limitations. For the essence of individuality is pride; and the desire to keep distinguishing characteristics is pride. So, the sixth degree is one of trembling and fear. It may take years and centuries to pass through this gate, but of a sudden it opens, and the flooding in of wider consciousness is known. This is the seventh degree. The cup is filled with the Elixir of Enlightenment, and he has seen the Holy Grail. The man who has reached this stage is henceforth an illuminated being and will gradually reap the fruits of illumination in his daily life.

After the seventh degree is reached a great veil must be passed before the real mysteries of the Trinity in Unity can be understood. But long before this the man has analyzed the Trinity in his own heart, and he has learned to look upon his substance as an ocean and his mind as the waves that traverse it. The cup has taught him to understand that in the last degree each particle is similar to all particles, and the diversity of the waves is the relation of the particles one to the other. The sense of relation or germ of intellectual comparison is the Great Mother Understanding. Her symbol is the Dove, carrying messages to and fro, the messenger which governs intellectual movements and defines the relation between one part and another. The origin of intellect is a definition of relation between the parts of the whole. Directly duality became possible a trinity became inevitable. When the two perceive each other comparison and relation arise as a third.

The last three degrees of meditation are mingled with these unspeakably tenuous ideas of ultimate unity. In the eighth degree the soul merges into the divine triad, the root of intellect, and becomes unified with the contemplated symbol; it itself is the Grail or container of the Divine Understanding; this is called the degree of ecstasy. The ninth degree of rapture is called the Divine Espousals, because the soul perceives its own absolute nature; the cup disappears and the separated nature passes into the unified nature leaving the soul in the simple absolute state which can perceive no differences; this is the tenth degree. The cup and the fire of love which melted it alike disappear. The virgin soul purified of all taint is crowned. This coronation of the Virgin is called by some the Divine Marriage because henceforward the soul cannot forget the nature of its ultimate state.

On the return from a meditation in which these ten degrees have been passed the soul experiences first rapture, then ecstasy, before its return to ordinary consciousness. It then becomes aware of a widely extended consciousness in which all things created and uncreated have a part. With anguish it sinks back into the individual state and passes through the degrees of peace, inebriation and quietude, and then once more aware of its body and the circumstances of its life meekly closes the shrine which contains the symbol of its blessedness and passes out into the world we live in.

In this example I have carefully compared the mystical theology of the Catholic Church and the Kabalistic degrees of the ten Sephiroth, and I think both these doctrines have been founded on the experiences of sane and accredited mystics. Scaramelli's book gives the process in far greater detail, and it has received the sanction of the Church of Rome.

There are other methods of using symbols to make impressions on our senses. For instance, the crucifix made with an oval center and limbs like a Maltese cross but with one prolonged as in the modern crucifix, appears in the carving on the walls of the Pyramid at Sakara, dating nearly 4000 B.C. It is used as a determinative for the word Nedz which is translated into Greek *soter*, or saviour. The later form of the hieroglyph is an upright pole with twisted cords forming the cross-beam. Egyptologists translate it "avenger," and it is applied to the son who avenges or saves his father from destruction. Horus is the great type of this work, and he saves his father Osiris from Set, his evil brother, who had put him to death and scattered his limbs throughout the land of Egypt. This crucifix was only used in the very early times in this relation, so that it is interesting that it should have emerged again three thousand years later as an emblem for the same redemptive idea in the symbology of the Christian Church.

The teachers of mankind who understood the value of association of ideas usually added the story of some popular myth to the symbol they intended to use, so that the sight of the symbol awakened the memory of the myth, and a hieratic allegory was later on constructed round the same symbol and communicated as the secret meaning to the initiated. It is true that to enjoin secrecy is one of the most effectual ways of impressing the memory, and the natural mind delights in analogy and will indulge in it as a fascinating pastime. It gives it a false sense of understanding the infinite; but it is very often a limitation to the real growth of the imagination. A priesthood which sets itself to weave folk stories into the ritual of religion gains great skill in working out analogies and uses the emblems of ideas it has woven into a discreet and orderly pattern to awaken the emotions and rouse the sleeping powers of the adolescents and sensitives under the discipline of its colleges.

The early cross was the symbol of the victorious Horus. He had fought with Set, the cruel brother of Osiris, the beautiful one. Set in some way represented activity and generation and Horus the sight of the seer. The result of the fight was that both gods were maimed, for it was no longer possible for Horus to see or for Set to generate. The blind Horus, however, was declared victorious and his sight restored. The Egyptians studied the art of self-control, and the first and most intimate enemy of self-control is the teeming mind which pours a stream of images before the vision. This must be sterilized by the seer resolutely closing his eyes to vision of any kind, and then Osiris rewards him by instructing him in the secret of his own liberation.

Another form of the cross called the Ankh, or symbol of Life, is found among the pottery marks of the first dynasty, and may date from the hypothetical age of Osiris himself, five or six thousand years before Christ.

The oldest form of the Ankh is the head of a man with the arms outstretched; but the hands are uplifted on either side of the face, in the attitude Moses assumed when he desired the children of Israel might overcome their enemies in battle. It is curious that these uplifted arms also represent the active part of the soul, or Ka, in the symbolic system of Egypt. The symbol of a head represents Horus— or Hru, as his name was spelt in Egypt— and the upright pillar was the Dad, or symbol of Osiris. It is called the backbone of Osiris and was associated with the practices of meditation on the minute central passage in the spinal cord.

We can analyze the symbol of life as a figure of a human being uniting the three elements represented by Horus, Osiris and Set. The head is Horus, the arms Set, and the body Osiris.

The body is the symbol of the idea of the Logos, or Name, the word Dad, and in the Pyramid texts we find it written out in full. It is identical with the word for "saying," "speech," or "Logos." Sometimes it is called the Tower of Flame or the blasting furnace-tower of Set-Hor. The Speech, or Osiris, united to the active generative power of Set and the insight of Horus, are the elements in the Egyptian cross or symbol of Life.

These three can be developed by training. Generation, becomes a power when it and its counterpart, imagination, are illuminated into the mystery of faith, for then there is a transubstantiation of the flesh. It rises in a great tidal wave and casts down all the closed gates and breaks the frame of the mind, so that the man becomes more than human. Thereafter no human law can measure his good and his evil, for it does not belong to the world of men. This wonderful and dangerous power of faith is one of the secrets that have always been guarded, but some of our geniuses have achieved it and some of our madmen have been shattered by it. Whence it comes or whither its goes cannot be told. Speech, in the same way, becomes a power when it is inspired and breathes beauty as an atmosphere to sense; for the word *Unnoufer*, the title of Osiris, means "beautiful being"; and he is the symbol of all beauty, and the Dionysian enthusiasm was the enthusiasm for the wine of Osiris, the spirit of beauty. Beauty is most active when she is enthroned in nature and awakens intuition and the love which covers a multitude of sins. Finally, sight, as Horus, is the symbol of wisdom, the eternal watcher, and under the ancient symbols of the gods Set, Osiris and Horus we perceive the whole symbol of Life to contain the three ways of the great ones: imagination and the arts and works; beauty and the qualities of perfection; insight, wisdom and philosophy.

The cross and circle have been handed down to us in various relations. Let us imagine the circle to mean insight and wisdom, the upright pole the Beautiful Being and the crossbeam to mean creation. Then let us interpret the progress typified by the change from the circle surmounting the cross shaped like the letter T, to the circle in the center of a Calvary cross and finally to the Greek cross surrounded by a circle. In the first instance the head, as a circle, symbolizes the wheel of the mind circling among the senses; in the second instance the wheel of the mind is centered in the region of the heart and the ideal of beautiful Being has reached upward to the head; the cross-bar also springs from the heart. We see in this change, the ritual of a spiritual progress in which the frame of the mind is broken and intuition, insight and imaginative faith satisfy the desire for instruction by words and experience, by vision and by works of generation. Dionysos has visited a man when he has passed through the telestic rites and unified the moods of his soul. Afterwards when the symbol is changed to the equal-armed cross within the circle a man learns the unity of the worlds and the circle of wisdom surrounds the equal armed cross of beauty and imagination. In the center of the earth which is the mystical omphalos, man has become united with nature and woven himself into the web of her various existences. He has found the symbol of the stone of the wise and realized its power in his own person.

In these changing crosses we must notice that the generative power of the imagination symbolized by the cross-bar passes from the place of the head to the heart and finally to the mystical omphalos; while the circle of wisdom passes from the head to the heart and finally outward till it surrounds the whole; and the beautiful Being alone remains unchanged in the midst. So, Osiris, being perfect in himself, remains the same, suffering the migrations of the two divine combatants Set and Horus. And Set, who rose up against him and hid him from the world in the storms of generative excess, is reduced through faith and devotion, or the way of the heart, to Being, or the way of the midst, the point of balance. Horus, by interchange of wisdom and imagination, is for a time blinded by the combat, but afterwards gains the perfect victory and becomes the boundary of the fullness of divine life.

The hierophants of the ancient mysteries, as I said before, delighted in these analogies and in the cruder analogies of puns and accidental resemblances which often appear to us quite meaningless unless we are willing to take a symbol into our own hearts and meditate upon it until it grows into a tree of life.

On the Play of the Image-Maker

The Latin word *ludo*, "I play" or "sport," is the root forming all such words as ludicrous, illusion, delusion, and so on. In Sanscrit the corresponding word is *lila*, and it is used to describe the work of creation.

We learn then, that it is the special work of the creative part of the mind to create delusive forms. I do not think we sufficiently realize that our life is in reality a series of illusions, and how much what we call our characteristics depend upon the bent of our illusions. For instance, if we accept the delusion that we are healthy, we overcome disease; if we are more open to the delusion that we are unhealthy, we give way before disease. This individual susceptibility to notions and impulses is the really interesting thing in the study of a human being. It does not arise from birthright and country. If it did twins would be identical. The theory of rebirth in numberless human forms does not explain the mystery, but only makes it more remote. The conscious mind has not much to do with it, nobody would consciously prefer to be in pain. The practical way of controlling it appears quite absurd; for it is not, as is sometimes asserted, will-power, but a kind of hypocritical pretense of believing what reason tells us is untrue. The assumption of an attitude of faith and the assertion of belief in words has over and over again been found to concentrate the unknown illusionary powers, and bring about some wished-for event.

This is one of the great puzzles of life. I remember years and years ago I was asked to regulate the beating of a hypnotized person's heart by saying aloud, "Your heart is to beat slower— a little quicker— that is right." I merely said the words without any assumed faith. I did not believe, I only said the words, and to my greatest astonishment the heart beat exactly as I told it to beat.

Effort, as commonly understood, has no effect comparable to this calm imperative statement. If a thing is really desired it cannot be attained, because real desire contracts and blocks up the passage of the words with emotion, or in some other unknown way. The law appears to be: There is nothing in the world you cannot do as long as you do not care whether it is done or not.

We have all seen this on the stage. We have seen one actor struggle and sweat over his part, and we have admired his devotion and intelligence. We have seen another peacefully expressing himself and the whole audience hanging on his words. The hard worker is generally getting £10 a week and the other £100.

Evidently calmness is a great power and desire a great weakness. A kind of mathematical precision is part of the expression of power; and I believe the faith in symbolic magic arises from the mathematical precision of symbols, because the contemplation of a perfect symbol gives perfect form to the imagination.

Let us consider the analogy between the imagination and the Demiurgos, or creator of the world. Because the symbol of the earth is imperfect it is said the creatures arising from it are liable to imperfection. The sphere of the earth is said to be flattened at the poles, and through some such bias in its form its laws and cycles are imperfect and vary unaccountably. The malformation is its individuality or personal character; and it is necessary to us to try and discover the laws of its lawlessness. They interest us.

In an old Sanscrit story the immortal bird sits with the mortal on the phantasmal Tree of Life, and the immortal does not eat of the fruits, but lives in contemplation. The mortal bird eats of the fruits, and they are joy and sorrow, life and death. A Vedic hymn tells how Death sits carousing with the gods at the foot of this tree, and the mortal who eats of the fruits is under the dominion of Death, who is the lord of the gods.

Why does the immortal Spirit sit twin-like beside the mortal and watch him live and die and fill himself with desire and satiety? It interests him. The link between the mortal and immortal brothers is so close, so terribly close, that throughout the life of the mortal the immortal feels unwillingness at the thought of separation.

I have heard people in the flush of health say that they do not care for the mortal side, and they would throw away their bodies as if they were old clothes. It would mean no more to them. It is an interesting mood. But only a mood. All mystics know that it is easy for an expert to enter the state of rigid trance voluntarily and to attain to a state of temporary death, in which the heart appears to stop beating. He may repeatedly and gladly leave his body but is he willing gladly to let his body leave him? I do not believe it.

I think the reason of this secret feeling of resentment against death is that the immortal bird has a certain satisfaction in watching his mortal brother, and the deep root of the sorrow of death and decay is this immortal regret. The mortal lie is a drama set up for the pleasure of the immortal witness; it often takes so deep an interest that tears fall from immortal eyes and cause wonders to appear on earth. The more miserable the story of the life the more exciting the drama becomes, and the less willing the immortal spectator is to say, "Enough." For that is all that is necessary to put an end to sorrow and decay and death and sin.

Why do we sit out these sordid dramas? Why does not our eternal consciousness retire from the contemplation of disease and cruelty? Can it be because it is tired of contemplation of eternal beatitude and perfection?

The oldest traditions say that is why.

Let us consider the question through our own feelings. When we first study philosophy, when we first open our eyes upon the world as baby children, we ask, "Why is everything happening?" Later on we say, "Why, if Unity is perfect, does creation arise from it?" The wise teacher replies, "You yourself came out from perfection; you separated yourself as a drop from the ocean, as a spark from the fire. Why did you do so?"

We wonder for a little, and then we remember it was because perfection and silence and unutterable bliss cannot be endured continuously; and so the immortal bird watches the sorrows of his mortal brother.

The absolute watches the relative, and it is his sport and play to do so.

So long as we consider ourselves as separate from this creator, the notion of being the sport of the gods is intolerable; and no human being in that stage of belief will hear of it with patience.

But when we have faced the appalling truth that we have ourselves constructed all that we know and remember because we chose to do so, we end by excusing ourselves. We know that we love in our hearts a rhythmical existence; we are willing to pass into trance, to attain consciousness of unconsciousness. We want to remember or forget at will, and let all the universe of suns and stars disappear in a flash. We want to be able to return; we do not want to be forced to return. We want to attain liberation and pass from the plenitude of the absolute into the deprivation of the relative without losing consciousness in the transitional states.

Again, there is a kind of drunken pleasure in this very loss of consciousness, and in sharing the delusions of the exterior world. We feel the inebriation of romance when we read about the "new knowledge" and the inevitable periods of elemental substances, of the shapely groupings of quivering particles. There is a triumph in the thought that little mortals have constructed means of measuring space and reckoning periods. But what does it matter really when we deep or die what laws may govern the exterior world ?

The only knowledge that could make a real difference to us would be the knowledge of how to enter into the consciousness that underlies these ultimate aggregations, these fiery dances of that primal state in which spirit and matter can no longer be distinguished from each other. The only thing of eternal importance is that we should be released from the notion that the particular groupings that we call our minds and bodies are the only groupings that make consciousness possible. We want to be able to understand and enter into the consciousness of simple organisms, of simple elements, and finally into the consciousness of universal life and its actions, desires and being.

How does any human soul attain this beatitude? Not because it can float in the ethers of the seven heavens, but because it has entered into the consciousness of further degrees in the scale of that simplification which ends in the knowledge of simplicity and wholeness united. The soul rests in the field of some larger knowledge than that represented by the ministers of visible nature.

We believe that the consciousness of organic life is diffused everywhere in temperate regions, and the Dionysian ecstasy of that consciousness comes to all who seek it faithfully in communion with organic life. The colder and more remote ecstasy of Apollo is that of the still more diffused consciousness of inorganic life. It is more ordered and less immediately destructive, although the passions of intense fiery energy blast the forms of organic life and fling them into a limbo of unconscious deprivation. For each degree of the mysteries must be attained slowly by delving into the last secrets of Being. How dear consciousness must be in these Apollonian regions of inorganic being, undogged by the slow motions of cells and the life they imprison! It can dart from sun to sun, seeing without eyes to blind it, hearing without the ears which deafen it to all but a little range of sounds. But before the ecstasy of Eros even the ecstasies of Apollo pass away, and in the blank etherial spaces the shining creators flit in the radiance that they themselves shed. All these ecstasies have been experienced by mystics who have described them over and over again. We need not wait till the whole world is fire and dew to know Dionysos and Apollo and Eros; they are all of them within reach of our hands, for they are the names we have given to states of the imagination and that which is beyond the making of images.

When we can attenuate our consciousness to the degree in which we can discern the substance of the stars, it is with us here. When we achieve this division or subdivision and realize that we can have a continuous consciousness woven through and through all degrees of substance, from the white life of the hottest star to the frozen death of the blackest moon, something is gained, and if the dream of existence is only a dream at least it will be free from the fears which make us sacrifice the noble aims, of life to the ignoble means of living. And if there is no other lie than this we are living now, to give a greater dream to others is better than to destroy and humiliate them in order that we may give alms to them and treat them with condescension. We cannot be great in the way of the world unless there are others who are small; we cannot be loved unless others are despised; we cannot earn unless others starve. But if our minds are great, then we shed a great blessing, for we no longer want anything which is limited; we do not want anything which others want, for we are satisfied by what we are in our own consciousness and do not need the possession and desires of the rest.

When we see this clearly we partake dimly in the play of the gods. We build up forms and watch them fade away. We initiate ideas which gradually start into life and fly on their own wings, and all the time we rest on the sure basis of the Gnosis which tells us form and sound will pass continuously into other forms and sounds, but the eternal Watcher remains. He is the immortal bird that does not eat of the tree of delusive life, but sits in its branches and sees them pass and fade and grow again in ever-varying form. He is God, and He is man when man has learnt to know who he is.

The Tetrad
or
The Structure of the Mind

The real man, otherwise the mind, whether it is the average mind deep in its own little groove or the supermind in touch with its race, has for characteristic, a power of passing from one state to another. The mind is a great actor, and the meanest intelligence is capable of recognizing that it can see all questions from many different points of view. To take a very obvious instance, a man respects the emotion of love when he feels it himself, but he professes the profoundest contempt for any other man who loves the same woman. He is therefore capable of seeing this passion at once as an ennobling and a degrading state; and he is able to compare the two points of view. He sees it from the center and he praises it. He sees it from the outside and he pours contempt upon it. In the same way the mental perceptions can look at all questions, from these two points of view, at least. The mental power of passing from the center to the circumference is analogous to the mental power of attaining absolute consciousness when the mind is stilled, and returning to relative consciousness when the mind is in motion.

I have already pointed out that we must consider the symbol of the absolute to be a mathematical point, and the symbol of the intelligence to be a triangle, or tetrad; because the intelligence deals with the relation between points, and not with the points themselves. This form of the tetrad, or a pyramid of three equilateral triangles, is the symbolic root of relative existence, or, in other words, nature. It contains four points and twelve possible relations, because each point stands in three possible relations to each other point. To understand this clearly it may be useful for a student to construct a magnified tetrad of points for himself with four marbles piled in a pyramidal form. We have taken the point itself as absolute consciousness; its relation with other points as relative consciousness; but its relations with one other point is said to manifest not as creation but as wisdom, an enlightening sympathy barren but resplendent, the aim of all philosophers. It is the relation of two perfectly wise beings rejoicing in perfection together.

Why does this inward and outward consciousness fall into the fatal act of creation? The answer of most traditions is "Because wisdom is also symbolically a serpent, and tempts to experiment." "Compare" is the fatal cry of the dual conscious mind; that is to say, the mind that can view itself from the interior or the exterior point of view. It has developed a power, and it wishes to use it. "Let me compare," it says. Then the third point, the power of criticism arises, and we have the subjective, objective and the spirit of comparison, which three form the fourth point, an opinion, or conviction. Each tetrad of consciousness is founded on its own particular conviction; and when we speak of fulfilling the law of our own being, we mean we must carry out our root conviction to its logical conclusion, and see it through all possible manifestations.

Mind, then, is the manifestation of what we call our identity or root conviction. This great Father in the Beyond takes on one form or another, but its insatiable will to experience and to compare devours all the endeavors of the little beings we, in an unenlightened state, call ourselves. The Father mind is the germ of relative consciousness arising as a phenomenon in dual consciousness, and all manifestations arise from it and its power of fixing the attention on certain patterns in the whole and rejecting others. In essential nature we are the infinite substance consisting of similar points, but we chose to limit our consciousness to the relation between certain parts of the whole, and to weave a pattern in the Cosmos. The great Father mind, or source of minds, is symbolized by the four lettered name of God by the Rabbis, as the Divine Tetractys or Chaturvyuha by the Brahmins, and with the little mind within each of us. We are all engaged in weaving smaller patterns that we may compare and judge of our experiences when we are drawn back into the fountain of being.

This happens every day. Each meditation is a Judgment-Day, each dream is a heaven or a hell, just as we have penetrated or not into the peace which passes understanding and comparison. In the *Bhagavat Purana* we find the mental faculties divided into four parts, making five phases in all, because the idea of the whole is added to the idea of the separated four parts. In Sanskrit the whole is called Antahkarana, really equivalent to the imagination, or image-maker, the creative power of the mind. The parts are called manas, buddhi, chitta and ahankara. Ahankara is the egoity of the image-maker, buddhi is the bias of the image-maker, chitta is the will of the image-maker, and manas the doubts and comparisons of the image-maker. The doctrine of the Vedanta is that egoity is the root of all delusions, because it deludes us into believing the temporal to be eternal and the eternal to be the temporal. The little self arranged or designed by the image, or patternmaker, takes upon itself the character of the unchangeableness of the points of eternal consciousness.

One aspect of the mind is the Logos, or famous four-lettered Name of many systems of symbology; the Dad, or Word of the Egyptians. Para, or the first aspect, is manifested in breath or Prana, *Sun*; Pasyanti, the second, in the mind, *Moon*; Madhyama, the third, in the powers of the mind; Vaikhari, the fourth, in articulate expression. These are analogous to the Rabbi's four methods of interpreting Scripture, through its rhythm, its melody, its phonetics and the literal meaning of the myths and fables used as methods of instruction. To paraphrase the Emerald Tablet, we may say that meditation on the word proceeds from the Sun-Father, or Prana, the Moon-Mother, or mind; the ten winds, or currents, carry it in their bosoms, and it is nourished by the earth, or physical sound of the name.

Close thought on the nature of the mind is a necessary part of the discipline of the mystic, for the mind is the bridge between the absolute and relative consciousness; it invites objective appearances to their invisible source through the subjective world.

In the *Bhagavat Parana* we read of the word that: "The Para division is said to be the latent sound, and is seated peacefully on the Serpent of Eternity as equilibrated will." The Pasyanti is the cause, or germ-thought, the Serpent that can dissolve all illusion and can cause all delusions; it is egoity. The Madhyama is friction making sparks. Sometimes it is the desire for complexity, or related consciousness, and sometimes the desire to return to simplicity, or absolute consciousness. It understands truly and falsely and is memory, doubt and sleep, buddhi, or judgment. Vaikhara is speech, and like melted butter can feed flame, as thought can feed desire.

The secret power of the word or mind sits as Vasudeva upon the Serpent and creation arises from him. The story is as follows:—

"When this universe was submerged in the waters of rest, the eyes of Vasudeva remained closed in sleep. He opened his eyes and saw himself lying on the Serpent King. He delighted in himself, remaining passive. Within him were all dreams and beings in latent being; only the power of time was manifest. Vasudeva dwelt as fire in wood with all his powers controlled, excepting only Time; having slept thus for 1,000 Yuga cycles, he found the lotuses of his body and the thread which unites them. That thread was pierced by Time and threw out energy, and, small as it was, it grew from his navel, and by the action of Time, which awakens law of cause and effect, it suddenly grew and became a lotus flower. Brahma was in that and looked on all sides (space came into being) and became four-faced, and he searched everywhere confused, and cried: 'Whence am I? Whence this lotus?' And he searched in vain. Then in his ignorance he began the work of creation."

Here we see the story of the mind of man, which despairs of discovering its own origin and creates images because it has no true wisdom. It cannot reduce itself to the dual state, which is omniscient, nor to the state of unity, which is Supreme until it has gained the power of comparison from experience.

We pass on to the Serpent mind which creates as egoity a World of images, the fuel of thought; then to the more familiar world of logical judgment, and finally to the world of speech where thought is expressed and manifested, as fire is made manifest in flame.

The Vedantic method of studying the nature of the tetrad as a symbol of the imagination, or mental power, is well described by Deussen in *The Religion and Philosophy of India*:

"When using the mind, senses and physical organs, a man believes his impressions of external objects of sense to be real (waking life); when only using the mind, apart from waking impressions, a man believes memories of these impressions to be real (dream); when the mind also rests, all consciousness of particular objects ceases and the man exists subjectively without conscious convictions of any kind (dreamless sleep); when the mind is gathered up by the consciousness and contrasted with all subjects and objects as undifferentiated substance it is set free from existing things and is in the state called liberation."

Now waking and dreaming are both states of delusion. In waking life, we reflect a manifold universe which has the same origin as ourselves. The perceptions of the waking life are obliterated in dream, and the perceptions of the dream life are obliterated on waking. We feel ourselves in bonds to both these conditions. We are surprised by what is done and said by others and by ourselves. We cannot control anything, because we are in bondage to our belief in the objective reality of these states.

There are two ways of dreaming. In the first the breath-father remains in its place and fashions a new world of forms from the material collected in its waking hours. In the other the breath-father forsakes the body and moves whither it will and sometimes finds difficulty in returning; it is said that the spirit wanders up and down in the garden of the body.

Of the state of deep sleep it is said: "Just as there in space a hawk or eagle folds its weary wings and drops to the ground after its circling flight, so the spirit hastens to the state where it knows no desire nor sees any dream-image, where the life breath is in union with thought."

But the yogi discovers a fourth state called Turiya. While awake and perfectly conscious he stills his mind as if in a brown study and commands it to go where he chooses, to cogitate on any problem he chooses, and to enlighten him on any subject he chooses, to build up for him the dream he prefers and to carry out his commands as a faithful servant instead of commanding him as a cruel tyrant.

The Western psychologist confesses his inability to compete with a yogi in the exercise of these faculties, which can be developed by an intelligent culture of the imagination. The Eastern writers (*until Deussen arose to interpret them*) have written in such obscure language that it is difficult for a Western mind to grasp that the mighty achievement they call "stilling the mind" has been familiar to us all in our childhood. Who among us has not, on being suddenly offered "a penny for his thoughts," found his mind to have been a complete blank or else an ecstatic fairy vision far removed from the understanding of his mortal companions?

The invariable reply is "I was thinking of nothing," or "My thoughts were far away."

Of course, if we sit down and say, "Now I will make my mind blank," the mere act of wondering whether we have made the mind blank prevents us from success, and it is here that the use of symbol comes as a boon to the struggling student of his own soul. Take the tetrad, the solid three-sided pyramid based on an equilateral triangle, and say: "I will meditate on this symbol of the fire-mind, I will think of the fire which melts thought into a molten mass and of the smith who hammers out forms." The mind, clinging to the symbol of its own primitive nature, the image whence sprang all imaginings, will hold fast to the meditation; it will next see itself in crystalline forms branching from the mineral into the vegetable symbolism; then in motion becoming animal in its nature and gradually, through comprehension of its own nature, becoming man as he will be when this object is accomplished. We are here in order that through experience we should learn to know ourselves. When we have accomplished this perhaps our minds may become mighty ghosts using the bodies of animals for our lower needs; or still more powerful and immortal as we learn that our bodies need never move, and that by the power of our imaginations all experiences are within us. I have already hinted that in those days when the world grows old and nothing but great forests can subsist, we, being part of the consciousness of earth, must accomplish a power that can act through the forms of life then possible. By degrees, as we melt once more into a cloud of fiery dust, the fire mind which has learned to understand the true nature of the crystalline life, that has followed its form back to the ultimate symbol of mind, can still retain its consciousness; for that symbol signifies the Eternal Relation eternally potential in the Eternal Absolute.

In this suggestion we see the idea behind the symbolism of the Tree of Life and the Philosophers' Stone. We in our natural state are so proud of belonging to the human species that we refuse to see what wonderful possibilities lie outside that form of life. But as we know, the ancient Egyptians realized the possibility of their divine ancestor, Osiris, manifesting through the form of a bull. The sacred animals of Egypt were provided with every means of leading a perfectly healthy physical life. Let us suppose a great mind exists in a ghostly body, but to impress its will upon the physical world it needs a dedicated vehicle, such as the body of an animal. The great mind, acting through the physical life of the purified animal, can function in a more manifest way than is possible to a mind bereft of all physical apparatus. The freshly killed animal offered before the Ka statue of a great ancestor, not so much as a sacrifice, but as a means of manifestation, was another form of this idea. Now we all expect a time to come when human life cannot be supported on this earth. It may become once more a land of dragons and amphibians. These creatures may develop a nervous system that can respond to and interpret consciousness even more rapidly than the human nervous system.

The idea that the simpler the form the truer the medium is not a new one. Mathematical truth is the only truth we can rely upon; crystalline form may be a far more subtle medium for revelation than organic form. The mysterious organ of the brain, which mystics say is the organ developed only by the highest of the human race, contains little sand-like crystallizations. Tree dryads may possibly be all the more active because their bodies are immovable, just as a yogi tells us that when his body is still as the dead his knowledge is clearest and his bliss is the most ecstatic.

The essential mind and the Stone of the Philosophers are the same, and its simplest form is the tetrad. The method of studying the mind by forcing the imagination to take certain forms is perhaps one of the most practical forms of mind-training that has ever been invented. It is especially useful to us in helping us to realize that we can dominate and alter form by application of the attention. Infinite possibilities of relative consciousness lie all around us, and through the use of mathematical symbols we can use and develop these elemental states of consciousness to the uttermost. We can combine them in infinite complications, and as long as we do not forget our own essential state we shall not be lost in the illusions of this world, or in the delusions of the madhouse.

Egyptian Use of Symbols

So many books have been published on the history, customs and religions of Egypt that I shall not attempt to say anything about the facts of the case. Anyone who cares to take the trouble can read about them elsewhere. What we want to do in order to get into touch with ancient Egypt is to imagine ourselves belonging to a nation that believed in the immortality of the soul and acted up to its belief.

The Egyptians believed everything that Europeans believe; but their faith was so great that it influenced their conduct in their public life and in their private relations.

The great believed that they literally were the sons of gods, for their fathers had invoked the god and had performed rites and made meditations and imagined overshadowings of divine natures before they were conceived. Marriage was a sacrament of most momentous nature involving long purifications and the communion with the Divine Trinities of Mother, Father and Child. Death was the consummation of initiation, and the regeneration of the body literally meant that the great initiates among them did believe that they could "take on" the forms of the soul at will and manifest to their representatives on earth in some shadowy substance whenever they desired to do so.

The descendants of the King offered sacrifices of living animals and fruits and wines on the days of the funeral, but they knew that thereafter the symbols or representations of these things would be sufficient for the purpose of the departed one. The kings had words written on the walls of their tombs telling of what had been offered to their subtle bodies (Ka), and they presented statues and pictures for the subtle body to permeate. The sensitive standing before such a statue and gazing into its eyes while he made offering to the manes of his ancestor seemed to see the form breathe and move while in his heart he knew the will of the great ancestor whose spirit had found union with the Superman Osiris. We offer flowers on the graves of our dead, but we do not communicate with them in our hearts; and the Egyptians did not do so either, unless the dead man or woman was an initiate who had learned to unite his powers and manifest upon earth or in the underworld at will.

The initiated Egyptian believed death involved the separation of the principles which united during incarnation to make an individual man. The rhythm of life and death appeared as a rhythm of union and separation. The will, appearing periodically as a compelling star, presided over birth and death, then faded back into the ether which was its substance. Under its influence, which was symbolized by the sun, a reflection arose symbolized by the moon, and together these powers formed the manifestation from the symbols of earth and air.

Ra, the sun, was the wine and sacrament, and Osiris, the earth, was the bread, and they united between the pillars of fire and cloud. Osiris was the lord of the underworld, opening and closing the gates of its separate chambers that Ra might pass through with the train of gods. And the idea of the initiate was that he should become one with Osiris, and make his manifestation on earth or climb up the ladder of heaven at will. The ladder was another symbol of the pillars. Set and Horus stood on either side of it, and when the initiate took an upward step he was united to Set, and when he stood upright on the step he was united to Horus. All this sounds very confusing, and it is still more confusing if read in the translations now obtainable. The only possible way of arriving at the solution of this symbolism is to apply it to the processes going on in the mental world. Every day we pass through all possible phases of consciousness. Broadly speaking they are deep sleep or unconsciousness; dreaming or thinking subjectively, without special reference to actions; and thinking and acting objectively or with regard to our surroundings and what we call facts. Deep sleep may be unconscious or it may develop into what has been called luminous sleep, or the heavenly state. The ladder which enables a man to reach the heaven world, or luminous sleep, is straight and narrow. By great will power, or concentration of the attention, it is possible to keep the balance between Horus and Set; that is to say, between the immortal fighters in the mind, which make the attention fall into an oblivious state or into the ceaseless wanderings of ordinary cogitation. These immortal fighters represent the subjective consciousness and the state of deep sleep. The inexperienced mind is always either wandering or unconscious; it has to fill itself with experience before it can watch and compare and harmonize the two states. When it has done so it realizes that in deep sleep or trance it is in a creative state, and prepares new combinations of its elements, and in the subjective state it is formulating these combinations and giving them definite form as thoughts. It is in the state called heavenly or luminous sleep that these things can be perceived. The man knows that he is one with his Creator and accepts the responsibility of that tremendous power. He becomes one with the Sun God in heaven; then with his train of creative powers he visits the Duat, or Underworld, which is the subjective world, or world of dream. Here he will find all the powers of the mental world, all the dreams and memories of the past, and all the plans and hopes for the future. It is a work-shop where the drama is prepared that will be acted upon earth.

The great difference between the earth and the Duat must be sought for in the difference between the physical life and the life of the mind. In the mind, or world of the Duat, the actor studies his part, he plans it, he consults with the creator or author, he receives impressions; in the physical world the play is produced, and the audience is impressed favorably or unfavorably. Manifestation of ideas takes place in visible form.

In Egypt the gods were everywhere worshipped, but the initiate was one with the gods. They represented the powers of the man who had realized that, by sacrifice of the little self, the great self was to be attained. This tremendous ideal is not a popular one. Innumerable seekers after truth recoil before the idea of losing their own individuality in the individuality of a perfect being. They would rather keep their own limitations than merge themselves in the unlimited.

It is just as if a drop of water desired to remain forever suspended as dew on the petals of a flower. It is separated, and it would rather evaporate in its struggle to keep its separate life than fall into the stream that is hurrying past to join the great ocean of consciousness. But I think we do not understand the nature of consciousness when we feel in this way. The Egyptians did.

Osiris represented to them the ocean of Human Consciousness, Ra the ocean of Cosmic Consciousness; and they realized that to enter into these beings was to attain plenitude and not to suffer deprivation. An individual consciousness as we know it is a partial consciousness. The subjective world has deprived itself of the consciousness of everything it calls the objective world. I am myself because I am different from all people and things; I can see around me. I am inferior to some and worship them by my love or envy; I am superior to others and pity them by my love or pride; and there are a very few whom I can look upon as real companions and comrades. In the same way with possessions, some are too good, some too bad and some are obtainable. Now this clinging to individuality is the great delusion which makes us so fatally interested in the state of being, as we are at present, mere aggregations of particles which are as aggregations incapable of immortality.

The moment we look at the question from outside we realize we should not like the present state of things to last forever. It is amusing to play the game, to pretend for a little while that we feel deeply about this or that; but directly we put it to the test and say to ourselves, "Do I want such and such a thing not only for a lifetime but forever?" we know very well we could not endure it. In our hearts we know that the charm of life is that it is ceaselessly changing. Even those who know the feeling of liberation from the delusion of delight in their own individuality, those who have lain down as Osiris, and entered into the shrine of Ra, even those will not seek the liberation of eternal contemplation. They cannot tear themselves away from the wheel of existence; they return, they say, to help the ignorant and guide the steps of the helpless. The wheel of change fascinates them; and the gods are delighted by the drama that ceaselessly unrolls itself before them. This was what the Egyptians felt. Deep in the center of the world of the Duat, in the navel of the wheel, dwelt Seker, the god who never moved. He had finished his course, and Ra cried to him at midnight, when his boat was towed within hearing of his abode in the depths of the Underworld.

Seker answered the cry of Ra, but none ever looked upon his face. In later times Osiris was shown in the form of a mummied hawk and was called Ptah-Seker-Osiris, and the supreme mystery of the adepts was hidden under this symbol. The mummied body fixed for ever in its eternal dwelling was the symbol of that central immovable point round which all changing things revolve. The illumination of the creative Sun-God passing through the great hierarchies of creation symbolized by the signs of the Zodiac was the wheel of Ptah, the opener or beginner of creation and the circle of the wheel. Osiris, the human being who had joined the alpha and omega of creation and passed from one to the other at will, represented the human desire to attain peace eternal, ameliorated by the possibility of change, even if it were merely the wheel of perpetual recurrence symbolized by the changing seasons of the year. So, Osiris is crucified on the spokes of the wheel in order that his consciousness may extend into the world of relative consciousness, or retire into the place of absolute consciousness at will. And the name of Ptah-Seker-Osiris was the symbol of this power of the human adept.

The Philosophy Called Vedanta

It will be seen that the Vedantists as well as the Kabbalists have used the idea of analogy and correspondences. For the threefold nature of the Holy Spirit corresponds to the threefold nature of the gods and of humanity. And the fivefold permutation of the ultimate divine state corresponds to the fivefold permutations of nature in her dark or automatic condition and to the fivefold per- mutations of the subtle body of a man.

We find that the fivefold nature of the Duat of the Egyptians and the fivefold Rose of the Rosicrucians bear the same interpretations; and the fivefold mystery is related to the Trinity, because, besides containing the separated qualities of the Trinity as the blossom, the fruit and the seed-pod, it contains them, united as it were, as three branches on one tree, and it contains them in their earliest potential state in the likeness of the seed before it is grown to a tree.

These states which we have already studied under the Kabalistic symbolism as the surrounding whirlings, the radiant center, and the separated Sephiroth; and again as the three pillars of the Sephirotic Tree, and as the king, queen and knight of the Tarot cards, are called in the Vedantic system *Sat*, or Being; *Chit*, or Wisdom, the Divine Sophia; and *Ananda* or Ecstasy. The *Sat-Chit-Ananda* is also regarded as a unity which had arisen from a former potential or seed-like state.

The state of rest is sometimes said to consist of a whirling so rapid that coherent form or relation is impossible, exactly as in ecstasy the saint is so preoccupied with the wonder of his own spiritual exaltation that no exterior power can affect him sufficiently even for him to be aware of its existence. After rest these wheelings of the spiritual ecstasy gradually slow down and by a long series of convulsive movements and sounds of thunder Nature brings forth from form her passion and her dancing.

The story of the birth of tangible things seems to be common to the East and to the West. But the peoples of the East do not attach the same value to our present life as the peoples of the West are inclined naturally to do. They have kept the external life so simple that they are able to face death with a splendid courage. We have made it so complicated and acquired excellence in the arts and sciences with so much toil that we feel a regret at parting with the mechanism we have educated and disciplined. We fear that we shall by some accident or foolish ignorance find ourselves astray when we wander among the shades on the banks of the dark river.

We do not love the simple ecstasy of nature as they do. They love the gift that cannot be taken from them; we love the passing glories of this world of painful civilization. They do not believe progress is an eternal reality. The greatest of their philosophers have looked upon life as a farce to be acted with as much forbearance as possible. We cannot do this; it is impossible for an un-philosophic mind to attain this attitude. And who is there with a philosophic mind here? We all have a touching faith in the value of our own work and wisdom. So, life in the East is seen to be an exquisite farce, and sometimes we have seen the dark mournful eyes of their princes watching our restless struggles and wondering that we should take so much trouble to disturb the world with our reforms. There is no object in living except to discover that living is a farce. What does it matter?

We can only mutter that these strange aloof beings who smile with sad eyes are mad. We are too much aware of our own worthiness. We deny that it is possible that the human race, and especially that part of it to which we belong, could have been created without a serious purpose; we fill life with serious purposes, and although we cannot do much for other people except give them mistaken advice, we still hope to find out something purposeful if we can only stay in the world long enough. I have said I have seen the sad eyes of a prince from the East wondering at the restless vulgarity of well-bred people. His face was of most wonderful perfection; and he said nothing, but moved about among the well-dressed rabble and went away quietly. Hours of instruction could not have taught me what the sight of that silent face stamped into my very soul: "I am here to learn to see through my own convictions. I am here to overcome the magician who has bewildered me. I am here to learn to know myself. That is the only purpose life has."

Another time I heard a certain Hindu philosopher, said by the late Professor Max Muller to be very learned; and although he seemed to think abuse more effective than argument, his conversation was very interesting. He had evidently been talking about her religion to a benevolent English lady. When I came into the room she was saying—

"There is something in all our hearts which makes us aspire to what is beyond."

The Hindu—That is all delusion and folly. You are ignorant of what man really is. You do not understand anything. These masters of religion you speak of are prophets whose work it is to enslave men. We, the teachers of the Highest come to free them from ignorance and delusion. We see down into the world of the prophets who bring religions into the world. No one can say, "I am the Son of God." God cannot be a father; that is a human relation. (Then in a thundering voice, he cried): I am beyond all gods. I am Atman. This body is nothing; the only body I have is infinite ecstasy.

The Lady—Yes, yes, that is all very well. But the God I speak of knows us and knows what we each require.

The Hindu—God does not know anything of the sort. His consciousness does not enter into the delusion of the foolish and ignorant. Oh, you are ignorant, you do not understand!

The Lady—Oh yes, I do; more than you think. I want something higher than you teach. I want the Kingdom of God, not of man.

The Hindu— I tell you, you are ignorant. You do not know what man is; you must go to hell.

The Lady—Oh, you believe in hell then?

The Hindu— Hell is being subject to delusions, and enjoying and suffering through the objects of delusion here. You will have to incarnate thousands and thousands of times.

The Lady— But I don't want to.

The Hindu—You will have to. You don't want to die, but you will die, and your dying thoughts will carry you into some other body— man, woman, fish, bird.

The Lady— I don't fear death.

The Hindu—Oh, you are ignorant; you cannot see that you are Infinite Spirit, all-pervading. I am That; you are That; she is That; he is That. There is no difference. That has no human relations; there is no father or mother or son about the matter.

The Lady— I believe in a God.

The Hindu—Millions of your fellow-countrymen have got beyond that; they know these religions are fables and delusions.

The Lady— Who died for me.

The Hindu— Martyrdom is a folly. It shows that a prophet does not know how to present his message. I should be a fool if I stood on the steps of your churches and said: "This is all wrong; pull down this place, this is all error." No, I speak to those who come to me for Truth. You had better go away.

After much persuasion she did go away. He was asked by someone else: "How did illusive power (Maya) contain the five elements of which Brahma is devoid?"

He replied: "In the Eternal Omnipresent Existence of Brahma the following five forms are contained: (1) Omnipresence; (2) Potential Power; (3) Illusion in Potential Power; (4) Knowledge; (5) Bliss. As long as an Omnipresent Knowledge of the Three in One exists, that Knowledge is Brahma. But when in the same Brahma a little atom becomes separately conscious of the idea of Bliss, then that atom's knowledge became an active God and the knowledge of Bliss an illusive power of God (Maya). The reflection of the knowledge of God in the Bliss became Jiva, or soul. It then forgot the knowledge of the Omnipresent Brahma and became an individual soul, and illusion was added to illusion and the five forms of Brahma emerged as the five elements we know. Salvation shall be for those who can recognize the reality underlying the illusive forms it dwells in."

This charming and naive statement of an ardent believer in the Divine state possible to human beings interested me at the time, but I found the philosophy was attended by a simplicity of nature so complete that it was impossible to forget my own experiences sufficiently to become equally simple.

It is very difficult to accept Eastern teaching as to the acting of the life-farce, although one is quite willing to admit that, theoretically, life is a farce. Sometimes one imagines that the ideal guru is not a messenger from the East but a certain radiant state of consciousness symbolized as the root with three branches, or the Omnipresent Knowledge of the Three in One.

There is little doubt that the mind has a visible and an invisible workshop. Like a great smith it hammers out problems and questions. This gives us the sensation of thought. We set ourselves to think out the best way to attack such and such difficulties. We clamor at the gates of some barrier. Suddenly, without any opening of gates, without any trouble at all we are there, we know all about the subject and we wonder that we should have asked a question when we knew the answer all the time. It is just as if part of us would insist upon fixing its attention on the mechanism of our ears instead of listening to the sound flowing in. Our mind is an instrument which asks questions, but cannot answer them. It is the receiver of answers just as our ears are the receivers of sound. We have only to focus our attention, for the Knower is within and without; it is not an individual reflection of Atman, but it is the universal Atman; but we clothe it in numberless forms of gods and spirits, gurus and fetishes.

The Omnipresent Knowledge of the Three in One of the creative, subjective and objective states of the soul is a center of radiance whence the three spring as illusionists, egoists and illusions, for egoism is the instrument of the illusionist. In the same way that the subjective mind is the instrument of the creative mind. The Omnipresent does not act in its state of union, but when separation takes place it appears as these phases of mind. Impulses bombard the personality and illusions are created because of the separated state of consciousness.

An hour ago, a simple instance of the difference between the wise and the foolish way of trying to accomplish something happened to me. I had been searching a book of some five hundred pages for a half-remembered passage for about five minutes in vain. I gave up the struggle and named the part of the passage I wished to find. My hands turned the leaves idly for half a minute and then the first finger of my left hand pointed to the exact passage. No act of superstition on my part, no intervention of spirits or guides was necessary. I only expressed my desire clearly and without agitation. A great many times I have found this process of the mind succeed. The questioning attitude, like the prayerful attitude is efficacious. It is the right one both with myself and other people; it is the right way to work the mind. A clear statement of the need in words is necessary. To tighten up the muscles and to clench the teeth in making a physical effort do not produce so good an effect as the loosening of the muscles in order to let power rush through the body. The force that flows through the nerves is gathered in from all sides, and if the flow is uninterrupted by violent contractions there is practically no limit to it, and power and knowledge come to us easily. But although many people have received illumination when the mind assuming its radiant form discovered to them its power and touched its own root, the state of Omnipresent Consciousness, they will not believe that so mighty a power can in reality attune itself to their petty human spirits. Like the English lady who talked of her God with confidence, they create illusive ideas for themselves and worship Omnipresent Consciousness as something outside and beyond them. To persist in this want-of faith in unity involves a fall deeper and deeper into delusion and separation, as the lady was warned by the philosopher, whose words she could not understand.

The root of the delusion of progress is in this want-of faith. We can all ask questions now; we need not wait for some indefinite future. Ask the question and listen to the answer which comes in the form of an idea without apparent process of thought or logic. It is true that after the idea has come, the logical faculty delights to play with it and examine its perfections. For logic is always useful as a means of convincing ourselves that what we have made up our minds to do is right. Logic is the plaything of the mind and slowly goes over the ground that the radiant mind traversed in the millionth of a second.

When a few people meet together and ask trivial questions while they tilt a table, they succeed in getting answers because the least common measure of their minds is capable of answering foolish questions foolishly. If their purpose and questions are on more important matters the least common measure may be of a higher quality. But it is very seldom that two or more can think out high problems better than one in solitude after concentration and meditation; for these practices are the best means for stilling thought and hearing wisdom.

It is possible that a guru and his chela, whose natures are specially attuned to each other, may produce thought and expressions of thought impossible to either of them alone, especially when the two are filled with devotion. For the questions of one stimulate the higher mind of the other. The guru can answer any intelligent question put to him, and the oracles of the ancient world were examples of this very common power; for it is an almost universal experience with teachers of all sorts that they can often give extraordinarily clear replies on subjects they had not considered beforehand when an intelligent pupil asks them a sufficiently definite question.

Socrates stimulated himself by the questions he asked, and it is a strange thing that the method is not more freely used in the elementary discipline of the mind practiced by all who seek to know themselves. There is an interchange between all who ask and all who answer as subtle as the interchange between an orator and his audience. He gives them words; they give him life; and each quickened pulse desiring light feeds his eloquence with a more brilliant inspiration.

On the Kabbalah

The mind is orderly and it revels in the law of correspondence, and the Kabbalah is perhaps the most elaborate revel the mind of man has ever held. The letters of the alphabet were systematized in the worlds of number and sound. Each represented number and an idea, and the numerals themselves were arrangements, or qualities, or hierarchies, or worlds formed from the division of ideal unity.

Preceding number were the three states of negative existence, corresponding to the state of a seed. These are called Nothingness— Unlimitedness— and Limitless Light.

The ten first numbers are attributed to ten divine qualities, ten archangels, ten hierarchies, ten worlds and innumerable demonic beings and worlds. The six first numbers are arranged at the corners of a hexagram, the four last in a Calvary cross. I will not go further into details of the correspondence of the ten numbers, for the four letters of the Holy Name must now be woven into the four worlds, and the ten Sephiroth multiplied into forty, each world corresponding to an element and a plane.

It was possible to reduce every number from one to forty to its exact correspondence and equivalent; and not only this but every letter of the Hebrew alphabet carried the same symbolism after another manner. It was all stately and elaborate, and previously I have given more details of the ideas connected with it and one plate from the rare fourth volume of Rosenroth's *Kabalah*. But in this place, I will only speak of the kind of symbolism such a system implies.

If it were founded on some tangible correspondence, such as the chemist, Mendelejeff's *Periodic Law,* it is easy to see that it would be the key to the rhythm of physical and mental states. We can imagine a thread of memory carrying our consciousness back to the ultimate unity of the first Sephira and emerging from that into the complexity of physical life by elaborate and coherent arrangements of particles. The ultimate structure of atoms may very probably be revealed eventually as following some definite law of the kind as elaborately repeated in more and more complex patterns as the temperature is reduced. If so, one who has studied the details of the Kabalistic system as described in the works of Reuchlin and Pico della Mirandola will be able to apply the principles he has learned to the actual facts of science. He will have no difficulty in admitting that the root of mind and body are both to be found in the simple states of prima materia. The thread of memory will carry him from the Form to the Formless, and he will realize the possibility of passing to and fro from the material to the formative, from the formative to the creative, and from the creative to the archetypal worlds, in an elaborate gymnastic of the mind. The body is the Garden of Eden and the Tree of Life in the midst are the ten Sephiroth. They are the key of life also and are arranged, in the form of a circle surmounting a cross, not unlike the symbol of the planet Venus.

The symbol may be taken to represent the aureole of forces surrounding the man within the man. We read of this Being in the Upanishads as the man in the heart, the size of a thumb. He is the conscious Being within us and can move from place to place by an effort of attention. The configuration of the Sephiroth shows the relative stations of the Universal and the Individual, and the interplay of the internal and the external life breaths or Sephiroth.

I think enough has been said to show that Jacob Boehme and William Blake were inspired by the same desire to construct a system of correspondences as the elaborators of the Kabbalah. It is a kind of revel of the mind, of no interest to anyone who has not become obsessed by the idea of construction. I do not think that the Kabalistic system works, but I believe the Jews lament this and attribute it to the loss of the Word which legend says was stolen from the Temple.

We still have traces of the old methods of divination by means of the Kabbalah in our playing cards, and more especially in the Tarot pack of seventy-eight cards, which consists of groups exactly corresponding to the symbols of the Kabbalah.

They are as follows :—

>Four suits of ten, corresponding to the ten Sephiroth in the four worlds.

> Four suits of court cards, kings, queens, knights and valets, corresponding to the letters of the name in the four worlds.
>
> And in addition twenty-two trumps corresponding to the twenty-two letters of the Hebrew alphabet.

I should point out here that nearly all the games we play, such as chess, draughts and cards, are founded on mediaeval magical systems. And it seems more than probable that they were originally invented for the purposes of divination. Indeed, one can look back to a period when drama originated from the ritual of the Mysteries and painting from the construction of talismanic images which should protect or avenge the owner, whether they were painted on his walls or earned in an amulet hanging from his neck-chain. Song was the sounding of mantrams, or evocatory ejaculations. Poetry was a spell made potent by its rhythms and meters. We have passed from this solemn world of superstition and eternal communion with supernatural beings, through the arts, into another world. We no longer believe in the consciousness of anything but ourselves. We answer our own puzzle as to the origin of consciousness by saying that in its early stages, it is irritability and chemical reaction. These are ugly words, and the thought is ugly. Perhaps we shall learn more about it if we wait a little while. We may find that Life is a beautiful creature after all, even when she is only fiery passion and shows herself in detonations and convulsions and in sudden flame and in sullen smoke.

The Kabalistic system is the foundation of most of the Theurgic formulas that were practiced in the Middle Ages. They are dangerous to the student because, although we are safe in endeavoring to attain to the Being of God, strange terrors beset us on every side the moment we try to understand the supernatural powers of the ministers of God. Iamblichus defends Theurgy on the ground that the Egyptian hierophants practicing it had themselves become supernatural beings. Theurgy may be said to be a right practice when the consciousness has been able to penetrate the consciousness of other species. A priest, limited to the experience of his own species, attempting to practice Theurgy for the small advantages of a special race, enters into the battle-field of nature with no equipment against disaster, and invites madness and misfortune, because that kind of smallness means a want of understanding of his own invulnerability or, I might call it, his own ultimate degree of being, which is the ultimate degree of the Being of Nature. The fool who is forbidden to use the practices of Theurgy is the fool who stands apart from life, himself an isolated spectator of its panorama; this is the ignorance which is death. Under the law, sin is folly and folly is sin, and the fool is battered and tortured until he learns wisdom. In order to try and grasp the idea of the ultimate unity which is within us all now and here, after the Kabalistic fashion, let us use the symbol of the mathematical point. Let us picture to ourselves all the forms we know resolved into their last essence; that is, into an infinite quantity of points of exactly similar appearance. When we have called up this idea in our mind let us imagine a consciousness in each of these points, but it must be purely a consciousness of a self-sufficing nature, a feeling of plenitude and well-being united to the certainty that space only contains similar beings to itself and time can produce no real change in its nature. This is called, I think, by all mystics the consciousness of oneness, the solitude which is the source of every change in time and space. The center is everywhere and the circumference nowhere.

Let us again picture to ourselves the infinite number of points arranged as a honeycomb so as to take up the most compact relation possible. Now the idea of circumference comes into existence. Magnified on the flat we see one surrounded by a circle of six or three points surrounded by a circle of nine or two by a circle of eight. (I will not attempt to confuse matters by going into the relation of solids; I am imagining a surface of points merely for the sake of clearness). We begin, therefore, with a relation of one surrounded by six, two surrounded by eight, and three surrounded by nine. We must now imagine a consciousness, arising in the units, of a relation to other units. That is to say, interest or inquiry is awakened; the consciousness is no longer at peace in the assurance of its own omnipresence and plenitude; it becomes aware that it is in relation to other units. It is no longer all-sufficing, and the idea awakens in it that in addition to its own ineffable being there exist, potentially within it, innumerable powers of combination. Alone, it is surrounded by six possible relations. United to one other it is surrounded by eight potencies, or means of power. United to two others it is surrounded by nine potencies.

When this idea arises the point enters into relation with other points and becomes a line, a triangle, a cube and all the variety of created things, because its attention is transferred from the contemplation of the all-sufficing nature of pure consciousness to the contemplation of the endless variations of related consciousness. Consciousness of relation is the stirring of the Great Breath. The arising of intelligence from the intelligible substance does not change it any more than drops of water change when the waves pass through the ocean. The points are there unchangeably and eternally the same; but mutual relations arise, now here and now there, as the breath of life, or desire, passes from one to the other in curves or angles of different kinds. So, it is with human consciousness, our attention is not fixed upon eternal substance until we search for it in the interior of our own sense of existence, but we are normally aware of consciousness as it relates us to our parts and to the history of our parts. We can even see it resembling the shadow coil of star dust we call a nebula or the embryo of a universe. We watch it churning and circling until the magic glamour makes us imagine that solid bodies come into existence as the whirling slows down.

To the Kabbalists the high part of the soul was in the state called *Yechida*, isolation and unity, symbolized by the absolute consciousness of similar points. In the point itself this changes into the relative state called *Chaya*, or life, and the soul was life long before it entered into the cup of *Neshama*, spoken of in the previous chapter. *Neshama* means literally the Aspiring One, and this part of the soul passes between the unified absolute consciousness and the relative consciousness of life. It gazes first at one and then at the other, and its love creates *Ruach*, the Inspired One, the Son of the Mother, *Neshama*. Finally, *Nefesh*, meaning breath or spirit, is the name given by the Kabbalists to the automatic part of the soul which carries on the functions of life. These parts of the soul correspond to the numbers 1, 2, 3, 6, and 9, and are supposed to reach the body through the head, the heart and the powers of reproduction. It is interesting to compare the Hindoo belief that the four principal castes took their origin from the corresponding parts of the body of Brahma, the Creator.

We perceive, therefore, that the Kabalistic Theurgists were well aware that two out of the five parts of the soul were on planes of consciousness in which the individual had no part. The link between these planes and the individual was the nature that aspires to life as a whole; that is to say, nature as the center which is everywhere. The two lower parts of the soul, *Ruach* and *Nefesh*, the inspired and the automatic, are of great interest; for *Ruach*, in its best sense, corresponded to the Messiah; it is complex, and is very nearly the same as the Antahkarana or interior creator, the image-maker of the Vedanta. It is the Egyptian Ka when it puts itself into the questioning attitude, before it becomes open to inspiration.

The *Nefesh* is reproductive, and repeats again and again the old ideas and the old circlings of the memory; but it is very important and can be taught to do almost anything by patient application. It appears to be incarnate memory; for it repeats what it has learnt, and appears to resent nothing except being required to give up old habits. It behaves like its prototype the number nine, which recurs eternally, and reduces all its multiples into the sum of itself. It is the force in us which clings to old paths, and explains new ideas by old platitudes.

Lastly in speaking of the Kabbalah as it has reached us we must remember that we have not received it from the Jews but from the Moors and the Italians and the Germans and the schoolmen of the Middle Ages. It is a cosmopolitan mixture of the ideas current in the fifteenth century, but it is far less interesting than other aspects of the same thought to which we will pass on.

The Rosicrucians and the Alchemists

A legend arose in the time of the Lutheran outburst of a mysterious master called Christian Rosenkreutz, who was buried for a period of all years in the central cavern of the earth. His shrine was seven-sided, and all the symbols of the universe were said to have been found disposed round him in this place. The Egyptian tradition of Seker, the god in the central cavern of the Duat, evidently found an echo in the heart of the inventor of this legendary father of mysteries, and it will be interesting to try and discern the meanings of the main symbols of the Rosenkreutz legends in Egypt and in Germany.

The Egyptian Duat, or Underworld, was represented by a five-fold star, or star of five radiations, enlarging as they receded from the center, and therefore not bearing the same symbolism as the pentagram. The Rose is fivefold in its structure and is a well-known symbol of silence. The stages of its existence pass from the bud, or potential state of pralaya, to the unfolding of its leaves as the pleroma, or fulness or manifestation of creative power. Consciousness, thought, reasoning, will, and the sense of individuality are five of its powers; the five senses are other manifestations of the same symbol. When the pollen of a flower is ripe the creative work begins, the petals fall and the fruit and seed are formed. The processes of life are a rhythmic coiling and uncoiling; a radiation and attraction, and an emanation or separation. The fruit coils round the seeds, the juices pass to and fro, and finally the husk of the fruit bursts and the seeds fall out separately as emanations, each complete in itself.

So, in the degrees of human enlightenment the purest state is Being so unified and perfect that the kind of consciousness that depends upon comparison cannot exist. The second state is the sense of being without bounds, which is often called wisdom. The third state is discernment, or understanding, and may be attained by concentration of the subjective mind upon an object until full understanding is attained. And these states of the unmanifest consciousness are called Sat-Chit-Ananda in the Vedantic philosophy and Ain-Soph-Aur in the Kabalistic philosophy; and Ptah-Seker- Osiris was the concrete image of these ideas in Egypt.

Now the Rose of the Rosicrucians was a more complicated symbol than the Cup. As we have seen the Cup was a symbol of creation, and its form was connected with the symbol of a circle in contrast to the Cross. The symbol of the Rose contains five petals and five divisions of the calyx. It is evidently the symbol of creation in activity, not in potentiality only. Perhaps we may believe the Rose to be a symbol of the subtle body of man, which is one with nature, and the Cross the symbol of the body and the name of word of man. The union of the Rose and Cross would symbolize a man able to unite himself to the great powers of Nature, or tattvas, familiar to us under their Hindu names Akasa, Vayu, Tejas, Apas and Prithivi, or the kingdoms of sound, sensation, perception. absorption and reproduction more commonly called hearing, touching, seeing, eating and generating.

Now the notion of obtaining the natural powers of an adept is most apparent in the traditions that come through Egypt and Chaldea, and the idea of the super-essential state in contrast to power is most apparent in the Oriental traditions. The high caste Oriental has the aristocratic spirit that conceives the height of life on this world to consist in the delicacy of perception associated with perfect self-satisfaction, while the democratic spirit of the West cannot conceive itself without desires, struggles and potencies for gratifying desires; democracy wishes to do and to have; aristocracy is sufficient unto itself.

Rosicrucianism and Alchemy are both allegories constructed by these working democratic minds, and in the alchemical symbolism we can trace the exact degrees of initiation through which the man, still under the great race delusion of progress, must pass before he realizes that his real self is the same yesterday, today and forever.

It is true in a sense that this treasure of all sages, this knowledge of Being which all mystics seek, forms itself vehicles in time and space in which it carries out the imaginations which spring from the relative side of absolute consciousness, and it is interesting to trace the different degrees of attainment.

Alchemical symbolism is mainly the symbolism of distillation. To take a simple process, let us imagine that we desire to obtain the white and the red tinctures from honey. The alchemist would put the honey in the cucurbite of an alembic. Placing it over a gentle heat he would drive the essential part of the spirit into the head or beak of the alembic, whence it would pass as steam into the neck of the receiver and become liquid once more as it cooled. This liquid was the white tincture, or spirit of honey mixed with water. This is the symbol of that concentration and meditation whereby the mind of man becomes subtilized and fit to perceive philosophical impressions. The white tincture is the symbol of light and wisdom.

But to obtain the red tincture of power a far more complicated process had to be performed. It consisted mainly of pouring back the distilled spirit upon the black dead-head that had been left as residue in the cucurbite and by the exercise of great care and the addition of certain matters acting upon the mixture in such a way that finally the whole of the original matter was distilled and no black dead-head remained and a wonderful red tincture was the result of the transmutation of the black nature.

This symbolical process involves the passing through definite stages of progress in the world of changing life. Let us imagine it carried out to its logical conclusion upon our own earth. We know that the mineral kingdom is the state in which form lasts for infinite ages and can stand great heat and cold without destruction. We know that the giants of the vegetable kingdom last many hundreds of years, but although the process of their growth and decay is prolonged, they are not capable of resisting fire or of existing in the frozen zone. We know that certain animals, such as elephants, tortoises and parrots, live for very long periods of time. All these creatures have greater tenacity of existence in the forms or vehicles of life than the human creature.

It is also plain that as the earth becomes more and more subject to violent change, when the great floods and the ice and the burnings visit it, in its old age conscious life must exist in more enduring but less complex, sensitive, visible forms than it does at present. Now consciousness of Being is the name we give to the white tincture which the adept distils from his human form in the alembic of the mind. It is brought about by the fire of imagined emotion and devotion under the stress of intense concentration. To focus thought has the same effect as to focus sunlight. It becomes a force analogous to heat. It is, in a word, emotion evoked by the skill of the sage. In this fire the Adept raises his consciousness until it is separate from the gross body, and no longer aware of the objective world. Passing through the gate of dreams it enters the subjective world and lives in its own brightness. Here it learns that it can create infinite visions and glories, and here the saints rejoice, each in his own heaven. Here finally the sage perceives his own divinity and is united to his God. This is the white initiation in the eyes of the Rosicrucian doctors, and according to the scriptures of the alchemists the sage has gained the white tincture. The objective world only remains in his consciousness as blackness and ignorance and death. In his divine nature he seeks to redeem the dark world, to draw it up into the divine nature and make it perfect. His vision can now show him a world in which man can no longer exist in material human form. His own desire for wisdom has drawn up the human element out of the visible or objective state. He is no longer merely a man in a human body because his subtle body has possessed itself of the characteristic human faculty of self- conscious comparison, the origin of wit, laughter and criticism.

The humanity that is beyond animal consciousness has the power of acting and knowing at the same moment; it can seem one thing and know at the same time that it is another. It is not a noble quality; it is nothing more than the power of laughing at ourselves: and yet it is the great redeeming quality, for it is the germ of all wisdom and enlightenment.

The ordinary dreamer lives in his subtle body as the fool of his own fancy, and the dream shows how little human wisdom his subtle body has obtained: but the subtle body of an adept can perceive the illusionary formulation of panoramas of light and form arising from the half-seized impression of light falling at a certain angle across the red edge of a blanket and the linen of a sheet just as he closes his eyes. The dream of the sage is a consciously guided dream. Like an author, he writes his own dramas and delights in the joys and tragedies of his creation, He no longer suffers from the attacks and sorrows that his own mind creates, but observes them with excitement and interest. He watches his own tears and cuts into the heart of his own emotions.

These are some of the experiences of the sage who has transferred the human principle from the body of matter to the subtle body.

The material body may in this stage of enlightenment be considered as a beautiful and healthy animal; it carries on the physical functions in temperate ways, unaccompanied by the fantastic imaginations of a human being. And there is little doubt that the bull of Apis was considered to take the place of the body of the adept Osiris in this way. The body of a sacred animal would answer every purpose for the divine man whose invisible body had attained some degree of complex, conscious life. The nervous forces of the animal world act as the physical basis for the dream-powers of the subtilized or deified man.

In China the flying dragon, the mythical combination of all kinds of animal life, represents the body of the deified man that can command all the elemental states of matter that can exist in the air, the fire, the earth and the water. The dragon is the symbol of the material body of the being who has complete command of the elemental world and afterwards becomes the subtle body in the further stage of being of which we are told in Druid tradition.

When the earth grows older and complex animal forms such as flying-fish and sea-serpents and monstrous alligators, can no longer exist, another symbol must be taken from the writings of the Rosicrucian doctors and the alchemists, and we enter upon the study of the Tree of Life. He who eats of the fruit of the Tree of Life will become one with the Elohim, or creative gods, and will live for infinite ages.

Imagine the world enveloped in a great white cloud, moist and warm like a hot-house; giant palms and ferns and mosses dripping with moisture: a climate like that of the Cocoa-palm Islands off the west coast of Africa, where animals and men can only live a little time. In this world the adept would use some marvelous tree as the physical basis of his life: and his subtle body would have drawn up into itself all the forces of motion that make a tree less powerful to our minds than an animal. The subtle body in this state would have become a veritable dragon of complex forces. It would have drawn into itself the mixed sphinx-natures of the birds and the fish, the creeping things and the four-footed creatures. The dryad of each tree would be a mighty Druid; the great Pendragon would have his oak as a physical form and would exercise his power in reality as we can imagine the ancient Druid sages exercised theirs in imagination.

This state of the subtle body may perhaps have been symbolized by the Green Dragon of the alchemists, but the Red Dragon arose after still further distillation.

Now we have to imagine a world all fire and molten glory of flame, in which no tree or flower could exist; a world in which wonderful agate trees would circle the white crystals of their pith with bands of violet and hyacinth and blue melting into stretches of pale chalcedony and shrouded in dark crystal bark, their branches glimmering with emerald leaves; a world in which mineral life has learned at last to show itself in perfect form, where light and fire glowed alternately and played with elemental shapes and images of beauty. And so, at last, we come to the last symbol of the alchemists – the symbol of the final perfection, the Summum Bonum, the Philosopher's Stone.

Let us imagine what that state would mean for the adept; his gross body a pure ruby, a perfect crystalline form with all the powers of growth, of nourishment, of reproduction drawn from the vegetable kingdom into his subtle body, carried on without disgust or satiety through the beautiful mediums of fiery blossoms and shining leaves; his subtle body almost visible as a light shining in the fiery world; his children flowers of flame and his physical form an everlasting memory of beauty; his mind an all-pervading consciousness in which blossoming imaginations arose or subsided under the law of his will; a perception unified with a faculty that ordered joy to succeed sorrow and sorrow to succeed joy because he knew that one cannot manifest without the other. A supreme artist, he would rejoice in creation; a supreme critic, he would rejoice in contrast.

So, the red tincture would be attained and the black, the white and the red worlds explored and analyzed in the imagination of the Rosicrucians and alchemists of the Middle Ages.

We still see the same desire for progress among those who strive for the ancient stone here in this western democratic world of men who desire "to have" and "to do." But these circles of everlasting recurrence so dear to Friedrich Nietzche are not what he called them. They are not aristocratic.

The aristocracy of mind is shown in the philosophy of Villiers de l'Isle Adam, who cried: "As for living, our servants can do that for us." It is the feeling of the great Buddhist intellect who sees that in the words "I am not" there is a wonder and a vision and song far exceeding the mere ideas of limited ecstasy and knowledge concealed in the words "I am."

www.ingramcontent.com/pod-product-compliance
Lightning Source LLC
LaVergne TN
LVHW041634070426
835507LV00008B/623